GETTING TO KNOW THE WORLD'S GREATEST
INVENTORS & SCIENTISTS

STEVE
JOBS
&
STEVE
WOZNIAK

Geek Heroes Who Put the Personal in Computers

WRITTEN AND ILLUSTRATED BY MIKE VENEZIA

CHILDREN'S PRESS®
AN IMPRINT OF SCHOLASTIC INC.
NEW YORK   TORONTO   LONDON   AUCKLAND   SYDNEY
MEXICO CITY   NEW DELHI   HONG KONG
DANBURY, CONNECTICUT

Content Consultant: Matthew Turk, Ph.D., Professor of Computer Science, University of California, Santa Barbara

Reading Consultant: Nanci R. Vargus, Ed.D., Assistant Professor, School of Education, University of Indianapolis

Photographs © 2010: Alamy Images/INTERFOTO: 23; AP Images: 28 (Steve Castillo), 22 (Heinz Nixdorf Museumsforum), 30 bottom left, 30 bottom right (Paul Sakuma); Corbis Images: 3, 8 bottom (Bettmann), 11 (Ed Kashi), 26 top (Tony Korody/Sygma), 27 (Roger Ressmeyer); Getty Images: 30 top (Moshe Brakha), 29 (Acey Harper), 31 bottom (John Medina), 24 (Tom Munnecke); Peter Arnold Inc./Leonard Lessin: 8 top; Photo Researchers, NY/U.S. Army: 7; Retna Ltd./Kelsey McNeal/ABC: 31 top; Santa Clara University Archives/William C. Eymann Photograph Collection: 10; Smithsonian Institution, Washington, D/92-13442: 25; The Image Works/SSPL: 26 bottom.

Colorist for illustrations: Andrew Day

Library of Congress Cataloging-in-Publication Data

Venezia, Mike.
  Steve Jobs & Steve Wozniak : geek heroes who put the personal in computers / written and illustrated by Mike Venezia.
      p. cm. — (Getting to know the world's greatest inventors and scientists)
  Includes index.
  ISBN-13: 978-0-531-23730-4 (lib. bdg.)   978-0-531-22351-2 (pbk.)
  ISBN-10: 0-531-23730-3 (lib. bdg.)   0-531-22351-5 (pbk.)
  1. Jobs, Steven, 1955—Juvenile literature. 2. Wozniak, Steve, 1950—Juvenile literature. 3. Computer engineers—United States—Biography—Juvenile literature. 4. Apple Computer, Inc.—History—Juvenile literature. I. Title. II. Title: Steve Jobs and Steve Wozniak.
  QA76.2.A2V465 2010
  004.092'2—dc22
  [B]
                                      2009030214

8 9 10 R 19 18 17 16 15 14 13

Steve Jobs (left) and Steve Wozniak (right) developed the Apple II, the first successful home computer. This 1984 photograph shows the Apple cofounders and Apple president John Sculley with an Apple IIc.

On April 1, 1976, Steve Wozniak and Steve Jobs started up a company called Apple® Computer Inc. The two Steves, with some friends, assembled the first Apple **personal computers** in Steve Jobs's bedroom and his parents' garage. Only four years later, Apple was on its way to becoming one of the most successful companies in the world.

Even though both Steves were super
interested in electronics, their personalities
were totally different. Their combined strengths
made them the perfect team to start up a
groundbreaking **electronic computer** company.

Steve Wozniak was sort of shy. As a teenager,
for fun, Steve would spend hours and hours
in his room designing computers on big sheets
of paper. Steve Jobs was more outgoing and

restless. He was known to suddenly leave his
college classes or a job to search for answers
about the universe and the meaning of life. Once,
he even traveled to India, hoping to find answers
to **spiritual** questions that puzzled him.

What the Steves had in common was that
before most people even knew what a computer
was, both of them could imagine the future need
for computers in everyday life.

Stephen Gary Wozniak was born in 1950 in San Jose, California. Steven Paul Jobs was born in San Francisco, California, in 1955. When the two Steves were growing up, computers were huge machines used mainly by the U.S. government, large companies, and banks. Early computers were big enough to fill a large room. They could weigh more than 30 tons!

Banks and businesses used computers to solve numerical problems, store numbers, and keep track of customers' accounts. The army used computers to calculate the paths of artillery shells so they would reach their targets accurately.

This enormous ENIAC computer from the 1940s included around 19,000 vacuum tubes. Every day, several of these tubes would burn out and have to be replaced.

Early computers were so large because they needed thousands of **vacuum tubes** to control the flow of electricity that powered them.

Vacuum tubes like this one were used in the earliest computers.

Vacuum tubes look kind of like light bulbs. They got the job done, but they had lots of problems. Vacuum tubes broke easily, took up lots of space, and used lots of electrical power. They often overheated and burned out.

Then, in 1947, the **transistor** was invented, and everything began to change. Transistors served the same purpose as vacuum tubes, but they were tiny. Also, they could switch on and off as needed, so they weren't likely to overheat.

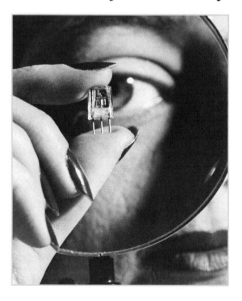

By using transistors instead of vacuum tubes, computers and other electronic devices could be made much smaller.

Transistors, like the one shown here, were much smaller and more efficient than vacuum tubes.

But even with transistors, hardly anyone could imagine that a computer could be made small enough to sit on someone's desk. People thought it was impossible. Luckily, geeks and engineers like Woz and Jobs didn't care what people thought.

Steve Wozniak grew up in Sunnyvale, California. Sunnyvale was in an area that became known as Silicon Valley. It was the perfect place to be if you were interested in becoming an **electrical engineer** and inventor. In the 1950s, all kinds of technology and electronics companies were opening up near Steve's home. The area was called Silicon Valley because scientists there had found ways to cram hundreds and thousands of transistors

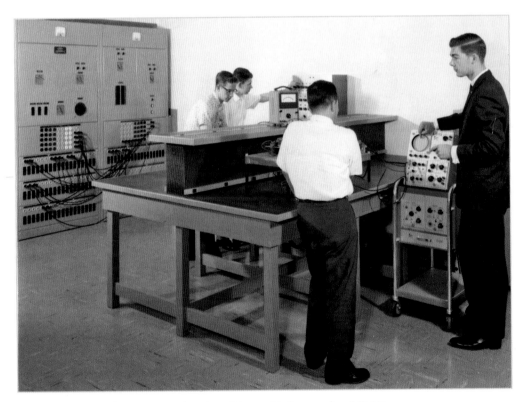

Engineering students at a school in Silicon Valley in the 1950s

Silicon Valley today

onto tiny individual **silicon chips.** These chips were able to run computers faster while taking up less space than ever.

Steve's father was an engineer who worked at an aircraft and rocket design company. Mr. Wozniak was an excellent teacher. He patiently answered every question his curious son asked. By the time Steve was eight years old, he understood all the basics of electronics.

Steve always loved making cool electronic gadgets. When he was in fifth grade, he came up with an intercom system that hooked up to five of his friends' houses. Late at night, the boys would secretly talk to each other. Their conversations were mostly about the new intercom.

Around the same time, Steve discovered some computer articles in his father's rocket science magazines. The articles were meant for high-level

government engineers, but Steve seemed to understand—*really* understand—everything in them. Steve thought the complicated descriptions and diagrams of early computers were the most exciting things he had ever seen. Throughout high school, Steve Wozniak was the star of his school's science fairs. He was always amazing teachers and parents with his science projects.

In 1968, after Woz graduated from high school, he went to the University of Colorado for a year. Then he attended a local college and got a job at a small computer company.

During this time, Woz and a neighbor and friend, Bill Fernandez, decided to build a computer. They worked hours on end, late into the night, in Bill's parents' garage. Bill and Woz drank tons of cream soda to keep themselves going. Because of this, they called their invention the Cream Soda Computer.

The Cream Soda Computer could only calculate answers to a few simple math problems. Even so, a local newspaper wanted to do a story about it.

Unfortunately, the computer had a total meltdown when the guys turned it on to show the reporter!

Woz wasn't upset, though. He was excited to have actually built a computer. He knew he could do better when he built the next one.

The Cream Soda Computer was important for another reason, too. It got Woz and Steve Jobs together.

Bill Fernandez went to high school with Steve Jobs. He knew Steve was also interested in electronics. One day, Bill invited Steve over to meet Woz and see the Cream Soda Computer. Steve Jobs was flipped out by Woz's knowledge of electronics. He and Woz got along really well. Woz thought Steve Jobs was one of the few people who really understood what he was doing.

Both Steves enjoyed sitting around
telling jokes and discussing rock music
and the latest electronics updates.

Steve Jobs, who was adopted as a baby by Paul and Clara Jobs, also grew up in Silicon Valley. Ever since he could remember, he had loved learning about electronic gadgets. Steve's dad was a **machinist.** As a hobby, Mr. Jobs would rebuild junk cars and sell them to make extra money. He often took his son along while he bought car parts. Mr. Jobs taught Steve early on how to bargain for the parts and make the best deal possible. This skill would come in handy later, when Steve Jobs started the Apple company.

Many of the Jobs's neighbors were engineers who worked for electronics companies. Steve wasn't afraid to bug them with tons of questions. One neighbor suggested that Steve join the Explorers' Club, a local club for kids interested in electrical engineering. Steve joined the club when he was ten. On one field trip, he got to see a room-size computer and how it worked. Steve was super impressed and wanted one for himself!

After the two Steves met, they each continued their schooling and then got jobs at different electronics companies. Woz also started attending a local electronics club called the Homebrew Computer Club. This club attracted a group of scruffy geeks who were crazy about the latest technology.

The Homebrew Club was very important. It was pretty much where the idea of people having home computers got its start! At meetings, everyone would talk about electronics and show each other gadgets they had made. Even though Woz was on the shy side, he felt right at home showing his latest projects to club members.

One day, Woz invited Steve Jobs along to a Homebrew meeting. There he presented the inner workings of what would become the first Apple computer. Everyone was amazed. Steve Jobs could feel the excitement. He knew right away that Woz was onto something big.

Tech fans loved the 1975 Altair 8800 because it was smaller than previous computers and came as a do-it-yourself kit. But it had major drawbacks. It had a hard-to-read front panel, no software, could only solve simple math problems, and had flip switches instead of a keyboard.

Steve Wozniak had created, for the first time, a small-sized computer that could be hooked up to a keyboard and TV screen. Woz typed a character on his keyboard, and club members saw a letter show up on the screen. This was a big deal. Up until this time, there weren't any computers with a screen or keyboard. Instead, you either had to slip a punch card into a computer or flip switches to enter information.

Answers were then displayed on rows of blinking lights instead of as numbers on a monitor. With Woz's computer, a person could program and receive information much more easily. The best part for Woz was that he would soon be able to program video games into his computer. Woz loved video games!

This 1976 photograph shows people playing Pong, one of the first video games, on a television screen. Steve Wozniak wanted to be able to play video games on a personal computer.

Steve Jobs stands in front of Apple's logo at a computer show in 1977.

Right away, Steve Jobs started talking to Woz about starting up a company to build and sell small, affordable computers. Both Steves were excited. They came up with "Apple" for the company's name because Steve Jobs thought apples were the perfect fruit and because he admired the Beatles' record label, which was also called "Apple." Steve Jobs got busy using his bargaining talent to make deals for expensive electronic parts.

He then found **investors** to lend the Apple company money so the guys could pay for the parts and hire workers to assemble computers. Steve Jobs also went out and got people interested in ordering the new Apples. The first order was from an electronics store, for fifty Apple I computers!

Apple's first computer, the Apple I, came without a keyboard, monitor, or case. This owner of this unit added a keyboard and his own wooden case.

Steve Jobs in his office at Apple Computer Inc. in 1981. At Apple, Jobs created a work environment where people dressed casually but worked really hard.

While Steve Jobs was getting the Apple company set up, Woz worked like crazy to improve his computer's design. Woz was a master of making the complicated inner workings of a computer smaller, while storing even more information. Woz designed the next Apple model, the Apple II, with a built-in keyboard. With the old Apple I, you had to buy and attach your own keyboard. The new Apple II was also capable of **high-resolution** graphics.

Jobs and Wozniak introduced the Apple II, the world's first successful personal computer, in 1977. It came with its own keyboard, included sound, and could display graphics in color.

The Apple II included sound and it had slots for game paddles, printers, and extra circuit boards. It came in a cool-looking plastic case instead of a clunky wooden one, and was ready to use right out of the box.

Steve Jobs continued making the Apple company more successful. He had a **vision** that soon, everyone would have a computer in their home. He knew computers were about to change the world, and he was determined to be the person to make that happen. And he was a different kind of leader—he wanted people at Apple to come to work in jeans rather than in business suits. He was known to walk around the place barefoot and in cut-off shorts.

In the 1980s, Wozniak kept improving the popular Apple II computer. Here he happily shows off an Apple IIe in 1983.

In the early 1980s, Steve Jobs led the engineering team that built the advanced Macintosh® computer. The Macintosh came with a mouse and used easy-to-read symbols, or **icons,** that represented programs. The Mac® was fun, easy to use, and inspired people's creativity. People couldn't wait to see what Steve Jobs would come up with next. With the success of the Apple II and the Mac, both Steves became super wealthy.

In 1985, Steve Wozniak decided to leave Apple. By then, Apple was a huge corporation. Woz didn't want to be part of a big company. He was more interested in starting up small companies. That way, he could do more of what he enjoyed most: coming up with cool product ideas that used the latest technology. For example, he invented and produced the first **universal remote.** Today Steve Wozniak enjoys founding museums and art centers. He also has fun teaching kids and organizing school computer labs.

Steve Wozniak loves to teach kids about computers. Here he's shown having fun with a group of middle-school kids who took part in an after-school computer class Steve taught in 1993.

Steve Jobs returned to Apple in 1997 and introduced the iMac in 1998.

Steve Jobs also left the Apple company for a while. He returned later, though, when Apple needed some help coming up with new cutting-edge products. Steve provided exactly what Apple needed. He was responsible for such super-popular products as the iMac®, iPod®, iTunes®, and iPhone™. Today, Steve Jobs is still inspiring workers at Apple and coming up with new product ideas all the time.

Steve Jobs has always wanted people to "Think Different." In recent years, he has taken the Apple company beyond computers, wowing customers with such popular products as the iPod (left) and the iPhone (right).

Early on, both Steve Wozniak and Steve Jobs were determined to change the way people gathered information and communicated with each other. They wanted their products to be easy to use and fun. When they started Apple Computer Inc. in 1976, hardly anyone knew what a computer was. Today, it's hard to imagine getting through the day without one.

Woz thinks life should be about having fun. In 2009, he even competed on the television show *Dancing With the Stars*.

In 2007, California governor Arnold Schwarzenegger honored Steve Jobs by inducting him into the California Hall of Fame.

Glossary

electrical engineer (i-LEK-tri-kuhl en-juh-NIHR) A person who designs electronics

electronic computer (i-lek-TRON-ik kuhm-PYOO-tur) A machine that can store and carry out lists of instructions called programs

high-resolution (HYE-rez-uh-LOO-shun) Having a high level of detail

icon (EYE-kon) A small picture on a computer screen that represents a program or function

investor (in-VEST-uhr) A person who gives money to a project in the belief that he or she will get money back in the future

machinist (muh-SHEE-nist) A person who runs or builds machines that make tools and parts

personal computer (PUR-suh-nuhl kuhm-PYOO-tur) A small computer that can be used by an individual at home, at school, or in an office

silicon chip (SIL-uh-kuhn CHIP) A miniature electronic circuit made of silicon, a material found in sand and rocks

spiritual (SPIHR-uh-choo-uhl) Having to do with the human spirit or soul

transistor (tran-ZISS-tur) A small electronic device that controls the flow of electric current in computers, radios, and many other electronics

universal remote (yoo-nuh-VUR-suhl ri-MOTE) A remote control that can be programmed to operate various brands of one or more types of electronic devices

vacuum tube (VAK-yoom TOOB) A tubelike device used to control the flow of electric current in computers, radios, and televisions before transistors were invented

vision (VIZH-uhn) A mental image of what the future will or could be like

Index